Thoughts and Coui

Saints for Every Day of the Year

Bonaventure Hammer

Alpha Editions

This edition published in 2023

ISBN : 9789357945400

Design and Setting By
Alpha Editions
www.alphaedis.com
Email - info@alphaedis.com

Contents

January

1

THERE are two guarantees of a wise rule of conduct: the thought before action, and self-command afterward.—ST. IGNATIUS.

2

When we receive with an entire and perfect resignation the afflictions which God sends us they become for us favors and benefits; because conformity to the will of God is a gain far superior to all temporal advantages.—ST. VINCENT DE PAUL.

3

All perfection consists in the love of God; and the perfection of divine love consists in the union of our will with that of God.—ST. ALPHONSUS.

4

Leave to every one the care of what belongs to him, and disturb not thyself with what is said or done in the world.—ST. THOMAS AQUINAS.

5

Place before your eyes as models for imitation, not the weak and cowardly, but the fervent and courageous.—ST. IGNATIUS.

6

Prayer is a pasturage, a field, wherein all the virtues find their nourishment, growth, and strength.—ST. CATHERINE OF SIENA.

7

A single act of resignation to the divine will in what it ordains contrary to our desires, is of more value than a hundred thousand successes conformable to our will and taste.—ST. VINCENT DE PAUL.

8

The shortest, yea, the only way to reach sanctity, is to conceive a horror for all that the world loves and values.—ST. IGNATIUS.

9

As long as we are in this mortal life, nothing is more necessary for us than humility.—ST. TERESA.

10

Learning without humility has always been pernicious to the Church; and as pride precipitated the rebellious angels from heaven, it frequently causes the loss of learned men.—ST. VINCENT DE PAUL.

11

Why remain sad and idle? Why exhaust thyself in the anguish of melancholy? Have courage, do violence to thyself; meditate on the passion of Jesus Christ, and thou shalt overcome thy sorrow.—BL. HENRY SUSO.

12

Here is the difference between the joys of the world and the cross of Jesus Christ: after having tasted the first, one is disgusted with them; and on the contrary, the more one partakes of the cross, the greater the thirst for it.—ST. IGNATIUS.

13

When the sky is free from clouds we can see more clearly the brightness of the sun. In like manner, when the soul is free from sin and the gloom of passion, it participates in the divine light.—VEN. LOUIS DE GRANADA.

14

Our works are of no value if they be not united to the merits of Jesus Christ.—ST. TERESA.

15

If we are very determined to mortify ourselves and not to be too much occupied with our corporal health, we will soon, by the grace of God, become masters of our bodies.—ST. TERESA.

16

In every creature, however small it be, we may see a striking image of divine wisdom, power, and goodness.—VEN. BARTHOLOMEW OF MARTYRS.

17

Time is but a period. It passes like the lightning flash. Suffering passes with time; suffering, then, is very short.—BL. HENRY SUSO.

18

In order to bear our afflictions with patience, it is very useful to read the lives and legends of the saints who endured great torments for Jesus Christ.—ST. TERESA.

19

Open thine ears to the voices of nature, and thou shalt hear them in concert inviting thee to the love of God.—VEN. LOUIS OF GRANADA.

20

On the feasts of the saints consider their virtues, and beseech God to deign to adorn you with them.—ST. TERESA.

21

When faith grows weak, all virtues are weakened. When faith is lost, all virtues are lost—ST. ALPHONSUS.

22

A precious crown is reserved in heaven for those who perform all their actions with all the diligence of which they are capable; for it is not sufficient to do our part well; it must be done more than well.—ST. IGNATIUS.

23

Nothing created has ever been able to fill the heart of man. God alone can fill it infinitely.—ST. THOMAS AQUINAS.

24

We should only make use of life to grow in the love of God.—ST. ALPHONSUS.

25

In vain men try. They can never find in creatures sincere affection, perfect joy, or true peace.—BL. HENRY SUSO.

26

God is supreme strength, fortifying those who place their trust and confidence in Him.—ST. CATHERINE OF SIENA.

27

God gives each one of us sufficient grace ever to know His holy will, and to do it fully.—ST. IGNATIUS.

28

Shun useless conversation. We lose by it both time and the spirit of devotion.—ST. THOMAS AQUINAS.

29

The upright intention is the soul of our actions. It gives them life and makes them good.—ST. ALPHONSUS.

30

The truth of faith alone, deeply graven in the soul, is sufficient to encourage us to very perfect works; for it strengthens man and increases his charity.—ST. TERESA.

31

It is folly not to think of death. It is greater folly to think of it, and not prepare for it.—ST. ALPHONSUS.

February

1

THE most perfect and meritorious intention is that by which, in all our actions, we have in view only the good pleasure of God and the accomplishment of His holy will.—ST. ALPHONSUS.

2

Mary's sorrow was less when she saw her only Son crucified, than it is now at the sight of men offending Him by sin.—ST. IGNATIUS.

3

There is nothing more unreasonable than to estimate our worth by the opinion of others. Today they laud us to the skies, to-morrow they will cover us with ignominy.—VEN. LOUIS OF GRANADA.

4

Act as if every day were the last of your life, and each action the last you perform.—ST. ALPHONSUS.

5

Perfection consists in renouncing ourselves, in carrying our cross, and in following Jesus Christ. Now, he who renounces himself most perfectly carries his cross the best and follows nearest to Jesus Christ is he who never does his own will, but always that of God.—ST. VINCENT DE PAUL.

6

That which would have easily been remedied at first, becomes incurable by time and habit—ST. IGNATIUS.

7

Among the gifts of grace which the soul receives in holy communion there is one that must be numbered among the highest. It is, that holy communion does not permit the soul to remain long in sin, nor to obstinately persevere in it.—ST. IGNATIUS.

8

Be assured that one great means to find favor when we appear before God is to have pardoned the injuries we have received here below.—VEN. LOUIS OF GRANADA.

9

Woe to him who neglects to recommend himself to Mary, and thus closes the channel of grace!—ST. ALPHONSUS.

10

It is folly to leave your goods where you can never return, and to send nothing to that place where you must remain for ever.—VEN. LOUIS OF GRANADA.

11

Discretion is necessary in spiritual life. It is its part to restrain the exercises in the way of perfection, so as to keep us between the two extremes.—ST. IGNATIUS.

12

By denying our self-love and our inclinations in little things, we gradually acquire mortification and victory over ourselves.—ST. TERESA.

13

Should we fall a thousand times in a day, a thousand times we must rise again, always animated with unbounded confidence in the infinite goodness of God.—VEN. LOUIS OF GRANADA.

14

God's way in dealing with those whom He intends to admit soonest after this life into the possession of His everlasting glory, is to purify them in this world by the greatest afflictions and trials.—ST. IGNATIUS.

15

After the flower comes the fruit: we receive, as the reward of our fatigues, an increase of grace in this world, and in the next the eternal vision of God.—BL. HENRY SUSO.

16

God refuses no one the gift of prayer. By it we obtain the help that we need to overcome disorderly desires and temptations of all kinds.—ST. ALPHONSUS.

17

To establish ourselves in a virtue it is necessary to form good and practical resolutions to perform certain and determined acts of that virtue, and we must, moreover, be faithful in executing them.—ST. VINCENT DE PAUL.

18

Love ought to consist of deeds more than of words.—ST. IGNATIUS.

19

There are many things which seem to us misfortunes and which we call such; but if we understood the designs of God we would call them graces.—ST. ALPHONSUS.

20

Let us abandon everything to the merciful providence of God.—BL. ALBERT THE GREAT.

21

Jesus Christ, our great Model, suffered much for us; let us bear our afflictions cheerfully, seeing that through them we have the happiness of resembling Him.—BL. HENRY SUSO.

22

Remember that virtue is a very high and rugged mountain, difficult to ascend, and requiring much fatigue and exertion before we arrive at the summit to rest.—BL. HENRY SUSO.

23

Labor to conquer yourself. This victory will assure you a brighter crown in heaven than they gain whose disposition is more amiable.—ST. IGNATIUS.

24

We should not examine articles of faith with a curious and subtle spirit. It is sufficient for us to know that the Church proposes them. We can never be deceived in believing them.—ST. VINCENT DE PAUL.

25

We should guard against jealousy, and even the slightest sentiment thereof. This vice is absolutely opposed to a pure and sincere zeal for the glory of God, and is a certain proof of secret and subtle pride.— ST. VINCENT DE PAUL.

26

Charity requires us always to have compassion on human infirmity.—ST. CATHERINE OF SIENA.

When one does not love prayer, it is morally impossible for him to resist his passions.—ST. ALPHONSUS.

28

Docility and easy acquiescence with good advice are the signs of a humble heart.—VEN. JULIENNE MOREL.

29

There is nothing richer, nothing surer, nothing more agreeable than a good conscience.—BL. BARTHOLOMEW OF MARTYRS.

March

1

IT SEEMS as if God granted to other saints to free us from some particular needfulness; but I know by experience that the glorious St. Joseph assists us generally in all our necessities.—ST. TERESA.

2

A most powerful and efficacious remedy for all evils, a means of correcting all imperfections, of triumphing over temptation, and preserving our hearts in an undisturbed peace, is conformity with the will of God.—ST. VINCENT DE PAUL.

3

It often happens that when we take less care of our body, we have better health than when we bestow upon it too much care.—ST. TERESA.

4

Do nothing, say nothing before considering if that which you are about to say or do is pleasing to God, profitable to yourself, and edifying to your neighbor.—ST. IGNATIUS.

5

Sometimes God leaves us for a long time unable to effect any good, that we may learn to humble ourselves, and never to glory in our efforts.— ST. VINCENT FERRER.

6

We easily lose peace of mind, because we make it depend, not on the testimony of a good conscience, but on the judgment of men.—BL. BARTHOLOMEW OF MARTYRS.

7

You may fast regularly, give alms, and pray without ceasing, but as long as you hate your brother, you will not be numbered among the children of God.—VEN. LOUIS DE BLOIS.

8

He who at the hour of death finds himself protected by St. Joseph, will certainly experience great consolation.—ST. TERESA.

9

Take care that the worldling does not pursue with greater zeal and anxiety the perishable goods of this world than you do the eternal.—ST. IGNATIUS.

10

We should consider our departed brethren as living members of Jesus Christ, animated by His grace, and certain of participating one day of His glory. We should therefore love, serve, and assist them as far as is in our power.—ST. VINCENT DE PAUL.

11

Control thy senses, guard thy mouth, bridle thy tongue, subjugate thy heart, bear all provocation with charity, and thou shalt perfectly fulfil the will of God.—BL. HENRY SUSO.

12

Our perfection consists in uniting our will so intimately with God's will, that we will only desire what He wills. He who conforms most perfectly to the will of God will be the most perfect Christian.—ST. VINCENT DE PAUL.

13

Humility, modesty, sobriety, purity, piety, and prudence, with meekness, ornament the soul, and make us live on earth a truly angelic life.—BL. JORDAN OF SAXONY.

14

In recalling to mind the life and actions of the saints, walk in their footsteps as much as possible, and humble thyself if thou canst not attain to their perfection.—ST. THOMAS AQUINAS.

15

When the devil again tempts you to sin, telling you that God is merciful, remember that the Lord showeth mercy to them that fear Him, but not to them who despise Him.—ST. ALPHONSUS.

16

In prayer we should particularly combat our predominant passion or evil inclination. We should devote continual attention to it, because when it is once conquered we will easily obtain the victory over all our other faults.— ST. VINCENT DE PAUL.

17

I will carefully consider how, on the day of judgment, I would wish to have discharged my office or my duty; and the way I would wish to have done it then I shall do now.—ST. IGNATIUS.

18

It is well to deny ourselves that which is permitted, in order to avoid more easily that which is not.—ST. BENEDICT.

19

I have noticed that all persons who have true devotion to St. Joseph and tender him special honor, are very much advanced in virtue, for he takes great care of souls who recommend themselves to him; and I have never asked of him anything which he did not obtain for me.—ST. TERESA.

20

He who forgets himself in the service of God may be assured that God will not forget Him.—ST. IGNATIUS.

21

Let all our actions be directed to the end that God may be glorified in all things.—ST. BENEDICT.

22

He who suffers in patience, suffers less and saves his soul. He who suffers impatiently, suffers more and loses his soul.—ST. ALPHONSUS.

23

When we remember or hear that the enemies of the Church burn and destroy God's temples, we should grieve therefor; but we should also rejoice much when we see new ones built, and we should co-operate in their erection as much as we possibly can.—ST. TERESA.

24

We should carefully beware of giving ourselves so completely to any employment as to forget to have recourse to God from time to time.—ST. TERESA.

25

Our Lady, deign to intercede for us sinners with thy divine Son, our Lord, and obtain of Him a blessing for us in our trials and tribulations!—ST. IGNATIUS.

26

Whoever would follow Jesus Christ, must walk in His footsteps, if he would not go astray.—ST. TERESA.

27

Let us thank God for having called us to His holy faith. It is a great gift, and the number of those who thank God for it is small.—ST. ALPHONSUS.

28

The trials of life cease to oppress us if we accept them for the love of God.—VEN. LOUIS DE GRANADA.

29

If you wish to take up your abode in the tabernacle of the heavenly kingdom, you must reach there through your good works, without which you can not hope to enter.—ST. BENEDICT.

30

It is a great folly to be willing to violate the friendship of God, rather than the law of human friendship.—ST. TERESA.

31

When the afflictions of this life overcome us, let us encourage ourselves to bear them patiently by the hope of heaven.—ST. ALPHONSUS.

April

1

TO PUT into practice the teachings of our holy faith, it is not enough to convince ourselves that they are true; we must love them. Love united to faith makes us practise our religion.—ST. ALPHONSUS.

2

Unite all your works to the merits of Jesus Christ, and then offer them up to the eternal Father if you desire to make them pleasing to Him.— ST. TERESA.

3

God pardons sin; but He will not pardon the will to sin.—ST. ALPHONSUS.

4

It is a fault, not a virtue, to wish your humility recognized and applauded.—ST. BERNARD.

5

Before engaging in your private devotions, perform those which obedience and your duty toward your neighbor impose upon you in such a manner as to make an abnegation of self.—VEN. LOUIS DE BLOIS.

6

The world is full of inconstancy; its friendship ceases the moment there is no advantage to be expected from us.—BL. JOHN TAULER.

7

There is nothing better to display the truth in an excellent light, than a clear and simple statement of facts.—ST. BENEDICT.

8

Be careful and do not lightly condemn the actions of others. We must consider the intention of our neighbor, which is often good and pure, although the act itself seems blameworthy.—ST. IGNATIUS.

9

He who does not overcome his predominant passion is in great danger of being lost. He who does overcome it will easily conquer all the rest.— ST. ALPHONSUS.

To conquer himself is the greatest victory that man can gain.—ST. IGNATIUS.

A soul which does not practise the exercise of prayer is very like a paralyzed body which, though possessing feet and hands, makes no use of them.— ST. ALPHONSUS.

When you do a good action, have the intention of first pleasing God, and then of giving good example to your neighbor.—ST. ALPHONSUS.

The grace of perseverance is the most important of all; it crowns all other graces.—ST. VINCENT DE PAUL.

Prayer is the only channel through which God's great graces and favors may flow into the soul; and if this be once closed, I know no other way He can communicate them.—ST. TERESA.

To acquire courage it is very useful to read the lives of the saints, especially of those who, after living in sin, attained great sanctity.— ST. ALPHONSUS.

The truly humble reject all praise for themselves, and refer it all to God.— ST. ALPHONSUS.

Prayer should be effective and practical, since it has for its end the acquisition of solid virtue and the mortification of the passions.—ST. VINCENT DE PAUL.

We do not keep an account of the graces which God has given us, but God our Lord keeps an account of them. He has fixed the measure thereof.— ST. ALPHONSUS.

19

The more guilty we are, the greater must be our confidence in Mary. Therefore, courage, timid soul; let Mary know all thy misery, and hasten with joy to the throne of mercy.—BL. HENRY SUSO.

20

Evil is often more hurtful to the doer than to the one against whom it is done.—ST. CATHERINE OF SIENA.

21

During life despise that which will avail you nothing at the hour of death.—ST. ANSELM.

22

He who fails to reflect before acting, walks with his eyes shut and advances with danger. He also falls very often, because the eye of reflection does not enable him to see whither his footsteps lead.—ST. GREGORY THE GREAT.

23

Sanctity and perfection consist not in fine words, but in good actions.—BL. HENRY SUSO.

24

As patience leads to peace, and study to science, so are humiliations the path that leads to humility.—ST. BERNARD.

25

Do not disturb yourself with vain curiosity concerning the affairs of others, nor how they conduct themselves, unless your position makes it your duty to do so.—VEN. LOUIS DE BLOIS.

26

The deceitful charms of prosperity destroy more souls than all the scourges of adversity.—ST. BERNARD.

27

The first degree of humility is the fear of God, which we should constantly have before our eyes.—VEN. LOUIS DE BLOIS.

28

He who cheerfully endures contempt and is happy under crosses and affliction, partakes of the humility and sufferings of Our Lord.—ST. MECHTILDIS.

29

He who is resigned to the divine will shall always surmount the difficulties he meets with in the service of God. The Lord will accomplish His designs concerning him.—ST. VINCENT DE PAUL.

30

Consent to suffer a slight temporary pain, that so thou mayst avoid the eternal pains which sin deserves.—ST. CATHERINE OF SIENA.

May

1

MARY was the most perfect among the saints only because she was always perfectly united to the will of God.—ST. ALPHONSUS.

2

After the love which we owe Jesus Christ, we must give the chief place in our heart to the love of His Mother Mary.—ST. ALPHONSUS.

3

When we feel our cross weighing upon us, let us have recourse to Mary, whom the Church calls the "Consoler of the Afflicted."—ST. ALPHONSUS.

4

The devotions we practise in honor of the glorious Virgin Mary, however trifling they be, are very pleasing to her divine Son, and He rewards them with eternal glory.—ST. TERESA.

5

There is nothing which is more profitable and more consoling to the mind than to frequently remember the Blessed Virgin.—ST. TERESA.

6

Blessed are the actions enclosed between two Hail Marys.—ST. ALPHONSUS.

7

Let us consider what the glorious Virgin endured, and what the holy apostles suffered, and we shall find that they who were nearest to Jesus Christ were the most afflicted.—ST. TERESA.

8

The servants of Mary who are in purgatory receive visits and consolations from her.—ST. ALPHONSUS.

9

If you persevere until death in true devotion to Mary, your salvation is certain.—ST. ALPHONSUS.

10

He who remembers having invoked the name of Mary in an impure temptation, may be sure that he did not yield to it.—ST. ALPHONSUS.

11

Mary being destined to negotiate peace between God and man, it was not proper that she should be an accomplice in the disobedience of Adam.—ST. ALPHONSUS.

12

Mary having co-operated in our redemption with so much glory to God and so much love for us, Our Lord ordained that no one shall obtain salvation except through her intercession.—ST. ALPHONSUS.

13

He who wishes to find Jesus will do so only by having recourse to Mary.—ST. ALPHONSUS.

14

Mary having always lived wholly detached from earthly things and united with God, death, which united her more closely to Him, was extremely sweet and agreeable to her.—ST. ALPHONSUS.

15

Mary being in heaven nearer to God and more united to Him, knows our miseries better, compassionates them more, and can more efficaciously assist us.—ST. ALPHONSUS.

16

The Virgin Mother, all pure and all white, will make her servants pure and white.—ST. ALPHONSUS.

17

To assure our salvation it does not suffice to call ourselves children of Mary, therefore let us always have the fear of God.—ST. TERESA.

18

Let us offer ourselves without delay and without reserve to Mary, and beg her to offer us herself to God.—ST. ALPHONSUS.

19

Such is the compassion, such the love which Mary bears us, that she is never tired of praying for us.—ST. ALPHONSUS.

O Queen of heaven and earth! The universe would perish before thou couldst refuse aid to one who invokes thee from the depth of his heart.— BL. HENRY SUSO.

O most blessed Virgin, who declarest in thy Canticle that it is owing to thy humility that God hath done great things in thee, obtain for me the grace to imitate thee, that is, to be obedient; because to obey is to practise humility.—ST. VINCENT DE PAUL.

May the two names so sweet and so powerful, of Jesus and Mary, be always in our hearts and on our lips!—ST. ALPHONSUS.

Whatsoever we do, we can never be true children of Mary, unless we are humble.—ST. ALPHONSUS.

Let us highly esteem devotion to the Blessed Virgin, and let us lose no opportunity of inspiring others with it.—ST. ALPHONSUS.

As a mother feels no disgust in dressing the sores of her child, so Mary, the heavenly infirmarian, never refuses to care for sinners who have recourse to her.—ST. ALPHONSUS.

Each of our days is marked with the protection of Mary, who is exceedingly anxious to be our Mother, when we desire to be her children.—ST. VINCENT DE PAUL.

When the devil wishes to make himself master of a soul, he seeks to make it give up devotion to Mary.—ST. ALPHONSUS.

Let us have recourse to Mary; for of all creatures she is the highest, the purest, the most beautiful, and the most loving.—BL. HENRY SUSO.

29

Let the name of Mary be ever on your lips, let it be indelibly engraven on your heart. If you are under her protection, you have nothing to fear; if she is propitious, you will arrive at the port of salvation.— ST. BERNARD.

30

Know that of all devotions the most pleasing to Mary is to have frequent recourse to her, asking for favors.—ST. ALPHONSUS.

31

Let the servants of Mary perform every day, and especially on Saturday, some work of charity for her sake.—ST. ALPHONSUS.

June

1

CAN WE, amongst all hearts, find one more amiable than that of Jesus? It is on His Heart that God looks with special complacency—ST. ALPHONSUS.

2

One must wage war against his predominant passion, and not retreat, until, with God's help, he has been victorious.—ST. ALPHONSUS.

3

An act of perfect conformity to the will of God unites us more to Him than a hundred other acts of virtue.—ST. ALPHONSUS.

4

The love of God inspires the love of our neighbor, and the love of our neighbor serves to keep alive the love of God.—ST. GREGORY THE GREAT.

5

Live always in the certainty that whatever happens to you is the result of divine Providence; because nothing hard or laborious falls to your lot without the Lord permitting it.—VEN. LOUIS DE BLOIS.

6

Whatsoever good work you undertake, pray earnestly to God that He will enable you to bring it to a successful termination.—ST. BENEDICT.

7

What is a fruitless repentance, defiled almost immediately by new faults?—ST. BERNARD.

8

You propose to give up everything to God; be sure, then, to include yourself among the things to be given up.—ST. BENEDICT.

9

If you can find a place where God is not, go there and sin with impunity.—ST. ANSELM.

10

He can not err who is constantly with the visible Head which Jesus Christ has left to His Church, as its foundation, rule, teacher, and defender of the Faith.—ST. ALPHONSUS.

11

The more numerous the gifts we have received from God, the greater the account we must render to Him.—ST. GREGORY THE GREAT.

12

True penance consists in regretting without ceasing the faults of the past, and in firmly resolving to never again commit that which is so deplorable.—ST. BERNARD.

13

We are not raised the first day to the summit of perfection. It is by climbing, not by flying, that we arrive there.—ST. BERNARD.

14

What we do for ourselves during life is more certain than all the good we expect others to do for us after death.—ST. GREGORY THE GREAT.

15

Idleness begets a discontented life. It develops self-love, which is the cause of all our misery, and renders us unworthy to receive the favors of divine love.—ST. IGNATIUS.

16

Have death always before your eyes as a salutary means of returning to God.—ST. BERNARD.

17

If the devil tempts me by the thought of divine justice, I think of God's mercy; if he tries to fill me with presumption by the thought of His mercy, I think of His justice.—ST. IGNATIUS.

18

In time of temptation continue the good thou hast begun before temptation.—ST. VINCENT FERRER.

19

In the eyes of the sovereign Judge the merit of our actions depends on the motives which prompted them.—ST. GREGORY THE GREAT.

20

The benefits to be derived from spiritual reading do not merely consist in impressing on the memory the precepts set forth, but in opening the heart to them, that they may bear fruit.—VEN. LOUIS DE BLOIS.

21

As clouds obscure the sun, so bad thoughts darken and destroy the brightness of the soul.—VEN. LOUIS OF GRANADA.

22

To judge rightly of the goodness and perfection of any one's prayer, it is sufficient to know the disposition he takes to it, and the fruits he reaps from it.—ST. VINCENT DE PAUL.

23

To commence many things and not to finish them is no small fault; we must persevere in whatever we undertake with upright intention and according to God's will.—BL. HENRY SUSO.

24

The perfect champion is he who establishes complete control over his mind by overcoming temptations and the inclination of his nature to sin.—VEN. JOHN TAULER.

25

If the love of God is in your heart, you will understand that to suffer for God is a joy to which all earthly pleasures are not to be compared.—ST. IGNATIUS.

26

The world around us is, as it were, a book written by the finger of God; every creature is a word on the page. We should apply ourselves well to understand the signification of the volume.—VEN. BARTHOLOMEW OF MARTYRS.

27

A man of prayer is capable of everything. He can say with St. Paul, "I can do all things in Him who strengthened me."—ST. VINCENT DE PAUL.

28

Whilst here below our actions can never be entirely free from negligence, frailty, or defect; but we must not throw away the wheat because of the chaff.—VEN. JOHN TAULER.

29

Strive always to preserve freedom of spirit, so that you need do nothing with the view of pleasing the world, and that no fear of displeasing it will have power to shake your good resolutions.—VEN. LOUIS DE BLOIS.

30

Wo to us poor sinners if we had not the Divine Sacrifice to appease the Lord!—ST. ALPHONSUS.

July

1

HOW few there are who avail themselves of the precious blood of Jesus to purchase their salvation!—ST. IGNATIUS.

2

O Queen of heaven and earth! Thou art the gate of mercy ever open, never closed. The universe must perish before he who invokes thee from his heart is refused assistance.—BL. HENRY SUSO.

3

Our Faith will never be true unless it is united to that of St. Peter and the Pontiff, his successors.—ST. ALPHONSUS.

4

Short pleasures and long sufferings are all the world can give.—VEN. JOHN TAULER.

5

Learn to be silent sometimes for the edification of others, that you may learn how to speak sometimes.—ST. VINCENT FERRER.

6

Gratitude for graces received is a most efficacious means of obtaining new ones.—ST. VINCENT DE PAUL.

7

To a useless question we should answer only by silence.—ST. VINCENT FERRER.

8

We should not judge things by their exterior or appearance, but consider what they are in the sight of God, and whether they be according to His good pleasure.—ST. VINCENT DE PAUL.

9

Preserve purity of conscience with care, and never do anything to sully it or render it less agreeable to God.—ST. THOMAS AQUINAS.

10

Give not thyself too much to any one. He who gives himself too freely is generally the least acceptable.—BL. HENRY SUSO.

11

Affliction strengthens the vigor of our soul, whereas happiness weakens it.—ST. GREGORY THE GREAT.

12

To acquire purity of the soul, it is necessary to guard against passing judgment on our neighbor, or useless remarks on his conduct.—ST. CATHERINE OF SIENA.

13

Turn away the eyes of thy body and those of thy mind from seeing others, that thou mayest be able to contemplate thyself.—ST. VINCENT FERRER.

14

The brightest ornaments in the crown of the blessed in heaven are the sufferings which they have borne patiently on earth.—ST. ALPHONSUS.

15

We are not innocent before God if we punish that which we should pardon, or pardon that which we should punish.—ST. BERNARD.

16

Is there any one in the world who has invoked thee, O Mary, without having felt the benefit of thy protection, which is promised to those who invoke thy mercy?—ST. BERNARD.

17

It is the key of obedience that opens the door of paradise. Jesus Christ has confided that key to His vicar, the Pope, Christ on earth, whom all are obliged to obey even unto death.—ST. CATHERINE OF SIENA.

18

It is true that God promises forgiveness if we repent, but what assurance have we of obtaining it to-morrow?—VEN. LOUIS DE BLOIS.

19

We should offer ourselves and all we have to God, that He may dispose of us according to His holy will, so that we may be ever ready to leave all and embrace the afflictions that come upon us.—ST. VINCENT DE PAUL.

No one has a right to mercy who can not himself show mercy.—VEN. LOUIS DE GRANADA.

We should reflect on all our actions, exterior and interior, and before we commence, examine well if we are able to finish them.—VEN. JOHN TAULER.

The reason why the lukewarm run so great a risk of being lost is because tepidity conceals from the soul the immense evil which it causes.—ST. ALPHONSUS.

We should learn of Jesus Christ to be meek and humble of heart, and ask Him unceasingly for these two virtues. We ought, particularly, to avoid the two contrary vices which would cause us to destroy with one hand what we seek to raise with the other.—ST. VINCENT DE PAUL.

The sufferings endured for God are the greatest proof of our love for Him.—ST. ALPHONSUS.

It is in vain that we cut off the branches of evil, if we leave intact the root, which continually produces new ones.—ST. GREGORY THE GREAT.

How little is required to be a saint! It suffices to do in all things the will of God.—ST. VINCENT DE PAUL.

Wouldst thou know what thou art? Thou art that to which thy heart turns the most frequently.—VEN. BARTHOLOMEW OF MARTYRS.

When you covet that which delights you, think not only of the sweet moments of enjoyment, but of the long season of regret which must follow.—ST. BERNARD.

29

They who voluntarily commit sin show a contempt for life eternal, since they willingly risk the loss of their soul.—ST. GREGORY THE GREAT.

30

It suffices not to perform good works; we must do them well, in imitation of Our Lord Jesus Christ, of whom it is written, "He doeth all things well."—ST. VINCENT DE PAUL.

31

Put not off till to-morrow what you can do today.—ST. IGNATIUS.

August

1

CHRIST Himself guides the bark of Peter. For this reason it can not perish, although He sometimes seems to sleep.—ST. ANTONINUS.

2

Prayer teaches us the need of laying before God all our necessities, of corresponding with His grace, of banishing vice from our heart and of establishing virtue in it.—ST. VINCENT DE PAUL.

3

Take this to heart: Owe no man anything. So shalt thou secure a peaceful sleep, an easy conscience, a life without inquietude, and a death without alarm.—VEN. LOUIS DE GRANADA.

4

If you would know whether you have made a good confession, ask yourself if you have resolved to abandon your sins.—ST. BERNARD.

5

He who does that which is displeasing to himself has discovered the secret of pleasing God.—ST. ANSELM.

6

An ordinary action, performed through obedience and love of God, is more meritorious than extraordinary works done on your own authority—VEN. LOUIS DE BLOIS.

7

Vigilance is rendered necessary and indispensable, not only by the dangers that surround us, but by the delicacy, the extreme difficulty of the work we all have to engage in the work of our salvation.—VEN. LOUIS DE GRANADA.

8

Among the different means that we have of pleasing God in all that we do, one of the most efficacious is to perform each of our actions as though it were to be the last of our life.—ST. VINCENT DE PAUL.

9

I have to seek only the glory of God, my own sanctification, and the salvation of my neighbor. I should therefore devote myself to these things, if necessary, at the peril of my life.—ST. ALPHONSUS.

10

Idleness is hell's fishhook for catching souls.—ST. IGNATIUS.

11

Whoever imagines himself without defect has an excess of pride. God alone is perfect.—ST. ANTONINUS.

12

As we take the bitterest medicine to recover or preserve the health of the body, we should cheerfully endure sufferings, however repugnant to nature, and consider them efficacious remedies which God employs to purify the soul and conduct it to the perfection to which He called it.—ST. VINCENT DE PAUL.

13

To give up prayer because we are often distracted at it is to allow the devil to gain his cause.—ST. ALPHONSUS.

14

Curb the desire of display, and do nothing from human respect.—ST. VINCENT DE PAUL.

15

O Mary, vessel of purest gold, ornamented with pearls and sapphires, filled with grace and virtue, thou art the dearest of all creatures to the eyes of eternal Wisdom.—BL. HENRY SUSO.

16

We must be careful not to omit our prayers, confession, communion, and other exercises of piety, even when we find no consolation in them.—ST. VINCENT FERRER.

17

Let us leave to God and to truth the care of our justification, without trying to excuse ourselves, and peace will truly spring up within us.— VEN. JOHN TAULER.

18

Read good and useful books, and abstain from reading those that only gratify curiosity.—ST. VINCENT DE PAUL.

19

So great is the goodness of God in your regard, that when you ask through ignorance for that which is not beneficial, He does not grant your prayer in this matter, but gives you something better instead.—ST. BERNARD.

20

Men can use no better arms to drive away the devil, than prayer and the sign of the cross.—ST. TERESA.

21

He who knows well how to practise the exercise of the presence of God, and who is faithful in following the attraction of this divine virtue, will soon attain a very high degree of perfection.—ST. VINCENT DE PAUL.

22

One of the most admirable effects of holy communion is to preserve the soul from sin, and to help those who fall through weakness to rise again. It is much more profitable, then, to approach this divine Sacrament with love, respect, and confidence, than to remain away through an excess of fear and scrupulosity.—ST. IGNATIUS.

23

Let us remember that every act of mortification is a work for heaven. This thought will make all suffering and weariness sweet.—ST. ALPHONSUS.

24

Correction should be given calmly and with discernment, at seasonable times, according to the dictates of reason, and not at the impulse of anger.—VEN. LOUIS DE GRANADA.

25

There is nothing more certain, nothing more agreeable, nothing richer than a good conscience.—VEN. BARTHOLOMEW OF MARTYRS.

26

God, to procure His glory, sometimes permits that we should be dishonored and persecuted without reason. He wishes thereby to render us conformable to His Son, who was calumniated and treated as a seducer, as an ambitious man, and as one possessed.—ST. VINCENT DE PAUL.

27

All that God gives us and all that He permits in this world have no other end than to sanctify us in Him.—ST. CATHERINE OF SIENA.

28

If you can not mortify your body by actual penance, abstain at least from some lawful pleasure.—ST. ALPHONSUS.

29

One whose heart is embittered can do nothing but contend and contradict, finding something to oppose in every remark.—VEN. JULIENNE MOREL.

30

Without prayer we have neither light nor strength to advance in the way which leads to God.—ST. ALPHONSUS.

31

I have never gone out to mingle with the world without losing something of myself.—BL. ALBERT THE GREAT.

September

1

HE who perseveres with constancy and fervor will, without fail, raise himself to a high degree of perfection.—BL. HENRY SUSO.

2

An upright intention is the soul of our actions. It gives them life, and makes them good.—ST. ALPHONSUS.

3

You wish to reform the world: reform yourself, otherwise your efforts will be in vain.—ST. IGNATIUS.

4

Let all thy care be to possess thy soul in peace and tranquillity. Let no accident be to thee a cause of ill-humor.—ST. VINCENT FERRER.

5

Humility is a fortified town; it repels all attacks. The sight of it obliges the enemy to turn and flee.—VEN. LOUIS OF GRANADA.

6

The world is deceitful and inconstant. When fortune forsakes us, friendship takes flight.—BL. HENRY SUSO.

7

Perform all your actions in union with the pure intention and perfect love with which Our Lord did all things for the glory of God and the salvation of the world.—ST. MECHTILDIS.

8

An air of meekness and a modest speech are pleasing alike to God and men.—VEN. JOHN TAULER.

9

The saints owed to their confidence in God that unalterable tranquillity of soul, which procured their perpetual joy and peace, even in the midst of adversities.—ST. ALPHONSUS.

10

Look not to the qualities thou mayest possess, which are wanting to others; but look to those which others possess and which are wanting to thee, that thou mayest acquire them.—VEN. LOUIS DE GRANADA.

11

Your heart is not so narrow that the world can satisfy it entirely; nothing but God can fill it.—ST. IGNATIUS.

12

If you wish to raise a lofty edifice of perfection, take humility for a foundation.—ST. THOMAS AQUINAS.

13

It ordinarily happens that God permits those who judge others, to fall into the same or even greater faults.—ST. VINCENT FERRER.

14

Raise thy heart and thy love toward the sweet and most holy cross, which soothes every pain!—ST. CATHERINE OF SIENA.

15

Often read spiritual books; then, like a sheep, ruminate the food thou hast taken, by meditation and a desire to practise the holy doctrine found therein.—ST. ANTONINUS.

16

Love others much, but visit them seldom.—ST. CATHERINE OF SIENA.

17

God sends us trials and afflictions to exercise us in patience and teach us sympathy with the sorrows of others.—ST. VINCENT DE PAUL.

18

Armed with prayer, the saints sustained a glorious warfare and vanquished all their enemies. By prayer, also, they appeased the wrath of God, and obtained from Him all they desired.—VEN. LOUIS DE GRANADA.

19

All souls in hell are there because they did not pray. All the saints sanctified themselves by prayer.—ST. ALPHONSUS.

20

The thought of the presence of God renders us familiar with the practice of doing in all things His holy will.—ST. VINCENT DE PAUL.

21

If we consider the number and excellence of the virtues practised by the saints, we must feel the inefficiency and imperfection of our actions.— ST. VINCENT FERRER.

22

Prayer without fervor has not sufficient strength to rise to heaven.— ST. BERNARD.

23

The path of virtue is painful to nature when left to itself; but nature, assisted by grace, finds it easy and agreeable.—VEN. LOUIS OF GRANADA.

24

Always give the preference to actions which appear to you the most agreeable to God, and most contrary to self-love.—ST. ALPHONSUS.

25

As the branch separated from the roots soon loses all life and verdure, so it is with good works which are not united with charity.—ST. GREGORY THE GREAT.

26

We should constantly thank the Lord for having granted us the gift of the true faith, by associating us with the children of the holy Catholic Church.—ST. ALPHONSUS.

27

We should not spare expense, fatigue, nor even our life, when there is a question of accomplishing the holy will of God.—ST. VINCENT DE PAUL.

28

Some are unable to fast or give alms; there are none who can not pray.— ST. ALPHONSUS.

29

We meet with contradictions everywhere. If only two persons are together they mutually afford each other opportunities of exercising patience, and even when one is alone there will still be a necessity for this virtue, so true it is that our miserable life is full of crosses.—ST. VINCENT DE PAUL.

30

We should bear our sufferings in expiation for our sins, to merit heaven, and to please God.—ST. ALPHONSUS.

October

1

ALWAYS give good example: teach virtue by word and deed. Example is more powerful than discourse.—BL. HENRY SUSO.

2

If thou wouldst glory, let it be in the Lord, by referring everything to Him, and giving to Him all the honor and glory.—VEN. LOUIS DE GRANADA.

3

There is nothing more holy, more eminently perfect, than resignation to the will of God, which confirms us in an entire detachment from ourselves, and a perfect indifference for every condition in which we may be placed.—ST. VINCENT DE PAUL.

4

Prayer consists not in many words, but in the fervor of desire, which raises the soul to God by the knowledge of its own nothingness and the divine goodness.—BL. HENRY SUSO.

5

Let us make up for lost time. Let us give to God the time that remains to us.—ST. ALPHONSUS.

6

When thou feelest thyself excited, shut thy mouth and chain thy tongue.—BL. HENRY SUSO.

7

If it was necessary that Christ should suffer and so enter by the cross into the kingdom of His Father, no friend of God should shrink from suffering.—VEN. JOHN TAULER.

8

We should grieve to see no account made of time, which is so precious; to see it employed so badly, so uselessly, for it can never be recalled.—BL. HENRY SUSO.

9

Every time that some unexpected event befalls us, be it affliction, or be it spiritual or corporal consolation, we should endeavor to receive it with equanimity of spirit, since all comes from the hand of God.—ST. VINCENT DE PAUL.

10

There are some who sin through frailty, or through the force of some violent passion. They desire to break these chains of death; if their prayer is constant they will be heard.—ST. ALPHONSUS.

11

"Thy will be done!" This is what the saints had continually on their lips and in their hearts.—ST. ALPHONSUS.

12

He who would be a disciple of Jesus Christ must live in sufferings; for "The servant is not greater than the Master."—VEN. JOHN TAULER.

13

He who submits himself to God in all things is certain that whatever men say or do against him will always turn to his advantage.—ST. VINCENT DE PAUL.

14

If he be blind who refuses to believe in the truths of the Catholic faith, how much blinder is he who believes, and yet lives as if he did not believe!—ST. ALPHONSUS.

15

There is no affliction, trial, or labor difficult to endure, when we consider the torments and sufferings which Our Lord Jesus Christ endured for us.— ST. TERESA.

16

Outside of God nothing is durable. We exchange life for death, health for sickness, honor for shame, riches for poverty. All things change and pass away.—ST. CATHERINE OF SIENA.

17

If you would keep yourself pure, shun dangerous occasions. Do not trust your own strength. In this matter we can not take too much precaution.— ST. ALPHONSUS.

18

After knowing the will of God in regard to a work which we undertake, we should continue courageously, however difficult it may be. We should follow it to the end with as much constancy as the obstacles we encounter are great.—ST. VINCENT DE PAUL.

19

In your prayers, if you would quickly and surely draw upon you the grace of God, pray in a special manner for our Holy Church and all those connected with it.—VEN. LOUIS DE BLOIS.

20

Prayer is our principal weapon. By it we obtain of God the victory over our evil inclinations, and over all temptations of hell.—ST. ALPHONSUS.

21

We should never abandon, on account of the difficulties we encounter, an enterprise undertaken with due reflection.—ST. VINCENT DE PAUL.

22

Being all members of the same body, with the same head, who is Christ, it is proper that we should have in common the same joys and sorrows.—VEN. LOUIS DE GRANADA.

23

We should be cordial and affable with the poor, and with persons in humble circumstances. We should not treat them in a supercilious manner. Haughtiness makes them revolt. On the contrary, when we are affable with them, they become more docile and derive more benefit from the advice they receive.—ST. VINCENT DE PAUL.

24

Let not confusion for thy fault overwhelm thee with despair, as if there were no longer a remedy.—ST. CATHERINE OF SIENA.

25

As all our wickedness consists in turning away from our Creator, so all our goodness consists in uniting ourselves with Him.—ST. ALPHONSUS.

26

That which we suffer in the accomplishment of a good work, merits for us the necessary graces to insure its success.—ST. VINCENT DE PAUL.

27

We ought to have a special devotion to those saints who excelled in humility, particularly to the Blessed Virgin Mary, who declares that the Lord regarded her on account of her humility.—ST. VINCENT DE PAUL.

28

He who wishes to find Jesus should seek Him, not in the delights and pleasures of the world, but in mortification of the senses.—ST. ALPHONSUS.

29

Let us not despise, judge, or condemn any one but ourselves; then our cross will bloom and bear fruit.—VEN. JOHN TAULER.

30

It is rarely that we fall into error if we are humble and trust to the wisdom of others, in preference to our own judgment.—VEN. LOUIS DE BLOIS.

31

The best of all prayers is that in which we ask that God's holy will be accomplished, both in ourselves and in others.—VEN. LOUIS DE BLOIS.

November

1

WE SHOULD honor God in His saints, and beseech Him to make us partakers of the graces He poured so abundantly upon them.—ST. VINCENT DE PAUL.

2

We may have a confident hope of our salvation when we apply ourselves to relieve the souls in purgatory, so afflicted and so dear to God.—ST. ALPHONSUS.

3

The example of the saints is proposed to every one, so that the great actions shown us may encourage us to undertake smaller things.—VEN. LOUIS DE GRANADA.

4

Let us read the lives of the saints; let us consider the penances which they performed, and blush to be so effeminate and so fearful of mortifying our flesh.—ST. ALPHONSUS.

5

The greatest pain which the holy souls suffer in purgatory proceeds from their desire to possess God. This suffering especially afflicts those who in life had but a feeble desire of heaven.—ST. ALPHONSUS.

6

Death is welcome to one who has always feared God and faithfully served Him.—ST. TERESA.

7

True humility consists in being content with all that God is pleased to ordain for us, believing ourselves unworthy to be called His servants.— ST. TERESA.

8

The best preparation for death is a perfect resignation to the will of God, after the example of Jesus Christ, who, in His prayer in Gethsemani prepared Himself with these words, "Father, not as I will, but as Thou wilt."—ST. VINCENT DE PAUL.

9

The errors of others should serve to keep us from adding any of our own to them.—ST. IGNATIUS.

10

There is more security in self-denial, mortification, and other like virtues, than in an abundance of tears.—ST. TERESA.

11

A resolute will triumphs over everything with the help of God, which is never wanting.—ST. ALPHONSUS.

12

If humble souls are contradicted, they remain calm; if they are calumniated, they suffer with patience; if they are little esteemed, neglected, or forgotten, they consider that their due; if they are weighed down with occupations, they perform them cheerfully.—ST. VINCENT DE PAUL.

13

When we have to reply to some one who speaks harshly to us, we must always do it with gentleness. If we are angry, it is better to keep silence.— ST. ALPHONSUS.

14

The two principal dispositions which we should bring to holy communion are detachment from creatures, and the desire to receive Our Lord with a view to loving Him more in the future.—ST. ALPHONSUS.

15

In doing penance it is necessary to deprive oneself of as many lawful pleasures as we had the misfortune to indulge in unlawful ones.—ST. GREGORY THE GREAT.

16

In raising human nature to heaven by His ascension, Christ has given us the hope of arriving thither ourselves.—ST. THOMAS AQUINAS.

17

It is useless to subdue the flesh by abstinence, unless one gives up his irregular life, and abandons vices which defile his soul.—ST. BENEDICT.

No prayers are so acceptable to God as those which we offer Him after communion.—ST. ALPHONSUS.

19

It avails nothing to subdue the body, if the mind allows itself to be controlled by anger.—ST. GREGORY THE GREAT.

20

What is it that renders death terrible? Sin. We must therefore fear sin, not death.—ST. ALPHONSUS.

21

The Blessed Virgin is of all the works of the Creator the most excellent, and to find anything in nature more grand one must go to the Author of nature Himself.—ST. PETER DAMIAN.

22

If we would advance in virtue, we must not neglect little things, for they pave the way to greater.—ST. TERESA.

23

When one has fallen into some fault, what better remedy can there be than to have immediate recourse to the Most Blessed Sacrament?—ST. ALPHONSUS.

24

Afflictions are the most certain proofs that God can give us of His love for us.—ST. VINCENT DE PAUL.

25

Is it not a great cruelty for us Christians, members of the body of the Holy Church, to attack one another?—ST. CATHERINE OF SIENA.

26

The Church is the pillar and ground of truth, and her infallibility admits of no doubt.—VEN. LOUIS DE GRANADA.

27

He who truly loves his neighbor and can not efficaciously assist him, should strive at least to relieve and help him by his prayers.—ST. TERESA.

28

We should blush for shame to show so much resentment at what is done or said against us, knowing that so many injuries and affronts have been offered to our Redeemer and the saints.—ST. TERESA.

29

The reason why so many souls who apply themselves to prayer are not inflamed with God's love is, that they neglect to carefully prepare themselves for it.—ST. TERESA.

30

It is absolutely necessary, both for our advancement and the salvation of others, to follow always and in all things the beautiful light of faith.—ST. VINCENT DE PAUL.

December

1

IF WE consider all that is imperfect and worldly in us, we shall find ample reason for abasing ourselves before God and man, before ourselves and our inferiors.—ST. VINCENT DE PAUL.

2

No one should think or say anything of another which he would not wish thought or said of himself.—ST. TERESA.

3

We should study the interests of others as our own, and be careful to act on all occasions with uprightness and loyalty.—ST. VINCENT DE PAUL.

4

It is God Himself who receives what we give in charity, and is it not an incomparable happiness to give Him what belongs to Him, and what we have received from His goodness alone?—ST. VINCENT DE PAUL.

5

Let your constant practice be to offer yourself to God, that He may do with you what He pleases.—ST. ALPHONSUS.

6

It is not enough to forbid our own tongue to murmur; we must also refuse to listen to murmurers.—VEN. LOUIS DE GRANADA.

7

We can obtain no reward without merit, and no merit without patience.—ST. ALPHONSUS.

8

No harp sends forth such sweet harmonies as are produced in the afflicted heart by the holy name of Mary. Let us kneel to reverence this holy, this sublime name of Mary!—BL. HENRY SUSO.

9

The life of a true Christian should be such that he fears neither death nor any event of his life, but endures and submits to all things with a good heart.—ST. TERESA.

10

We should abandon ourselves entirely into the hands of God, and believe that His providence disposes everything that He wishes or permits to happen to us for our greater good.—ST. VINCENT DE PAUL.

11

Regulate and direct all your actions to God, offering them to Him and beseeching Him to grant that they be for His honor and glory.—ST. TERESA.

12

Conformity to the will of God is an easy and certain means of acquiring a great treasure of graces in this life.—ST. VINCENT DE PAUL.

13

Do not consider what others do, or how they do it; for there are but few who really work for their own sanctification.—ST. ALPHONSUS.

14

To-day God invites you to do good; do it therefore to-day. To-morrow you may not have time, or God may no longer call you to do it.—ST. ALPHONSUS.

15

To advance in the way of perfection it does not suffice to say a number of weak prayers; our principal care should be to acquire solid virtues.—ST. TERESA.

16

Humility is the virtue of Our Lord Jesus Christ, of His blessed Mother, and of the greatest saints. It embraces all virtues and, where it is sincere, introduces them into the soul.—ST. VINCENT DE PAUL.

17

It will be a great consolation for us at the hour of death to know that we are to be judged by Him whom we have loved above all things during life.—ST. TERESA.

18

Humble submission and obedience to the decrees of the Sovereign Pontiffs are good means for distinguishing the loyal from the rebellious children of the Church.—ST. VINCENT DE PAUL.

The devil attacks us at the time of prayer more frequently than at other times. His object is to make us weary of prayer.—BL. HENRY SUSO.

20

It is an act as rare as it is precious, to transact business with many people, without ever forgetting God or oneself.—ST. IGNATIUS.

21

God is our light. The farther the soul strays away from God, the deeper it goes into darkness.—ST. ALPHONSUS.

22

True Christian prudence makes us submit our intellect to the maxims of the Gospel without fear of being deceived. It teaches us to judge things as Jesus Christ judged them, and to speak and act as He did.—ST. VINCENT DE PAUL.

23

Remember that men change easily, and that you can not place your trust in them; therefore attach yourself to God alone.—ST. TERESA.

24

If we secretly feel a desire to appear greater or better than others, we must repress it at once.—ST. TERESA.

25

The King of heaven deigned to be born in a stable, because He came to destroy pride, the cause of man's ruin.—ST. ALPHONSUS.

26

To save our souls we must live according to the maxims of the Gospel, and not according to those of the world.—ST. ALPHONSUS.

27

Be gentle and kind with every one, and severe with yourself.—ST. TERESA.

28

If you wish to be pleasing to God and happy here below, be in all things united to His will.—ST. ALPHONSUS.

29

In proportion as the love of God increases in our soul, so does also the love of suffering.—ST. VINCENT DE PAUL.

30

He who keeps steadily on without pausing, will reach the end of his path and the summit of perfection.—ST. TERESA.

31

The past is no longer yours; the future is not yet in your power. You have only the present wherein to do good.—ST. ALPHONSUS.

————————————